Bald Eagles

By Dr. Hugh Roome

Children's Press®

An Imprint of Scholastic Inc.

Content Consultant
Nikki Smith
Assistant Curator, North America and Polar Frontier
Columbus Zoo and Aquarium

Library of Congress Cataloging-in-Publication Data

Names: Roome, Hugh, author.
Title: Bald eagles/by Dr. Hugh Roome.
Description: New York, NY: Children's Press, an imprint of Scholastic Inc., 2019. | Series: Nature's children |
Includes bibliographical references and index.
Identifiers: LCCN 2018003316| ISBN 9780531192597 (library binding) |
ISBN 9780531137529 (paperback) Subjects: LCSH: Bald eagle—Juvenile literature.
Classification: LCC QL696.F32 R65 2019 | DDC 598.9/43—dc23
LC record available at https://lccn.loc.gov/2018003316

Design by Anna Tunick Tabachnik

Creative Direction: Judith E. Christ for Scholastic

Produced by Spooky Cheetah Press

Printed in North Mankato, MN, USA 113

SCHOLASTIC, CHILDREN'S PRESS, NATURE'S CHILDREN™, and associated logos
are trademarks and/or registered trademarks of Scholastic Inc.

1 2 3 4 5 6 7 8 9 10 R 28 27 26 25 24 23 22 21 20 19

Scholastic Inc., 557 Broadway, New York, NY 10012.

Photographs ©: cover: Alan Murphy/BIA/Minden Pictures; 1: Serjio74/Dreamstime; 4 leaf silo and throughout:
stockgraphicdesigns.com; 4 top: Jim McMahon/Mapman ®; 5 child silo: All-Silhouettes.com; 5 top eagle silo: Lnmstuff/
Dreamstime; 5 bottom: Natural Planet/Pete Ryan/Media Bakery; 5 bottom eagle silo: Gpgroup/Dreamstime; 6 eagle silo and
throughout: draco77/iStockphoto; 7: David Osberg/Getty Images; 9: Chris Clor/Getty Images; 10: Alan Murphy/BIA/Minden
Pictures; 13: KenCanning/iStockphoto; 15: Patrick Frischknecht/Robert Harding Picture Library; 16: Klaus Nigge/Getty
Images; 19 top left: Yva Momatiuk and John Eastcott/Minden Pictures; 19 top right: Visuals Unlimited, Inc./Joe McDonald/
Getty Images; 19 bottom left: MikeLane45/iStockphoto; 19 bottom right: Jpiks1/Dreamstime; 21: Sylvain Cordier/NPL/
Minden Pictures; 22: Paul Nicklen/Getty Images; 25: Jeff Foott/Getty Images; 26: predrag1/iStockphoto;
29: Klaus Nigge/Getty Images; 31: James L. Amos/Getty Images; 32: Ondřej Prosický/Dreamstime; 35: Pete Ryan/Getty
Images; 36: USFWS Photo/Alamy Images; 39: Pgiam/Getty Images; 40: Andrew B. Graham/Getty Images; 42 bottom left:
Nature Bird Photography/Shutterstock; 42 top left: GlobalP/iStockphoto; 42 bottom right: 6381380/iStockphoto;
42 top right: SteveMcsweeny/iStockphoto; 43 top left: nicholas_dale/iStockphoto; 43 bottom: Neil_Burton/iStockphoto;
43 top right: Serjio74/iStockphoto.

Table of Contents

Fact File 4

CHAPTER 1 **Super Bird** 6
        Built to Hunt 8
        Claws of Steel 11
        High Fliers 12

CHAPTER 2 **Eagles Want a Beach House** 14
        Gone Fishing 17
        Also on the Menu 18

CHAPTER 3 **Becoming a Mom and Dad** 20
        Choosing a Home 23
        The Biggest Nest 24
        Egg to Eaglet 27
        Growing Up 28

CHAPTER 4 **Ancient Eagles** 30
        Seafaring Cousins 33

CHAPTER 5 **Eagles and Humans** 34
        Almost Extinct 37
        Ongoing Threats 38
        A Powerful Symbol 41

Bald Eagle Family Tree 42
Words to Know 44
Find Out More 46
Facts for Now 46
Index 47
About the Author 48

Fact File: Bald Eagles

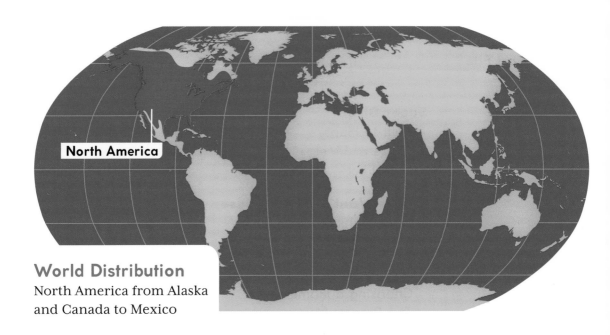

North America

World Distribution
North America from Alaska
and Canada to Mexico

Habitat
Live near water:
oceans, rivers,
lakes, and wetlands

Habits
Almost always
looking for fish
to eat; can fly to
great heights and
dive at high speed
for prey; mate
for life; build very
large nests

Diet
Mainly fish, but
also small land
animals and carrion

Distinctive Features
White head
and tail feathers,
with brown body
and wing feathers,
and bright yellow
beak and feet

Fast Fact
Bald eagles are
also known as
sea eagles.

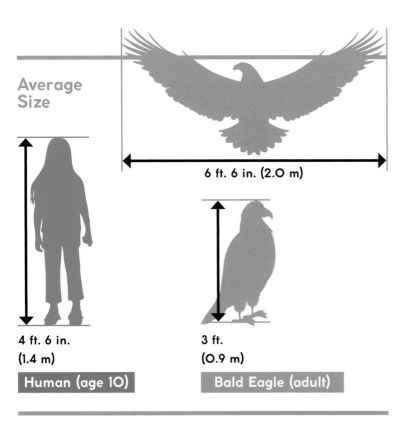

Average Size

6 ft. 6 in. (2.0 m)

4 ft. 6 in. (1.4 m)
Human (age 10)

3 ft. (0.9 m)
Bald Eagle (adult)

Classification

CLASS
Aves
(birds)

ORDER
Accipitriformes
(birds of prey)

FAMILY
Accipitridae
(raptors)

GENUS
Haliaeetus
(sea eagle)

SPECIES
Haliaeetus leucocephalus
(bald eagle)

◄ This eagle parent has brought part of a fish back to the nest for its chick.

CHAPTER 1

Super Bird

It is a cool, quiet morning in the Alaskan wilderness. Suddenly the silence is broken by the cry of a bald eagle. The giant **raptor** is flying high over a lake when she sees a fish far below. She dives down like a speeding bullet, spreads her huge wings to slow down, and grabs the **prey** in her claws. It is a large pike, a delicious dinner for her babies.

Many of the bald eagle's **traits** make this animal unique. It is one of the largest birds in North America. And it cannot be found anywhere else in the world. The bald eagle also has a very distinctive look. With its muscular body, white-feathered head, and bright yellow beak, there is no mistaking this bird for any other.

In 1782, the bald eagle was chosen as the symbol of the United States of America. The bird's great strength, long life, and incredible beauty seemed a fitting representation of the new nation.

▶ An eagle's razor-sharp claws deliver a killing blow.

Built to Hunt

Bald eagles are birds of prey—that means they are hunting birds. And their bodies are perfectly built for the task. These powerful **predators** stand about 3 feet (0.9 meters) tall. That's about as tall as a three-year-old child! A bald eagle weighs from 7 to 12 pounds (3.2 to 5.4 kilograms). Its favorite food is fish, and it does its hunting from above. The bird uses its keen eyesight to spot a fish from high in the sky. Then it dives down at super speed and snatches up the fish in its **talons**.

Fast Fact
Female bald eagles are 25% bigger than males.

Wings
can span up to 7 ft. (2.1 m); that's wider than an adult human is tall.

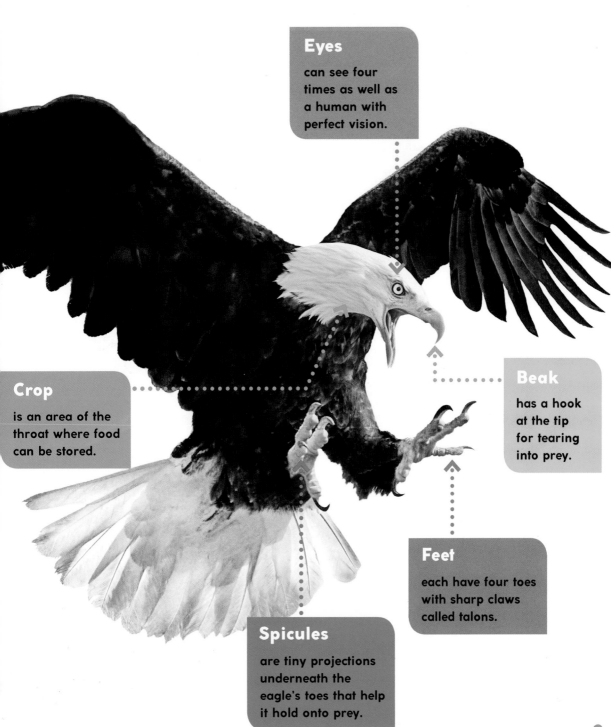

Eyes
can see four times as well as a human with perfect vision.

Beak
has a hook at the tip for tearing into prey.

Crop
is an area of the throat where food can be stored.

Feet
each have four toes with sharp claws called talons.

Spicules
are tiny projections underneath the eagle's toes that help it hold onto prey.

Claws of Steel

If you've ever seen a bald eagle up close, one of the first things you might notice is its large, bright yellow feet. The bird has four toes, each ending in a sharp claw called a talon. The talons are made of keratin, just like our fingernails. Three of the eagle's toes face forward, and one, called the hallux, faces backward. That helps the eagle grip things in its claws—and stay on its perch while it sleeps. Bald eagles can lock their toes around a branch so they don't fall out of the tree at night.

An eagle's talons are superstrong, enabling the bird to carry a fish that is half its own body weight while it flies at 30 miles (48.3 kilometers) per hour. Talons aren't just for carrying food, though. Like all birds of prey, the bald eagle kills with its feet. As the eagle grabs a fish, its sharp talons slice right through its victim's scales.

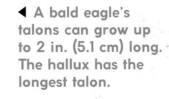

◀ A bald eagle's talons can grow up to 2 in. (5.1 cm) long. The hallux has the longest talon.

High Fliers

Bald eagles can fly as high as 10,000 ft. (3,048 m). Their feathers are light, but very strong. Eagles flap their wings to take off, but they often **soar** through the sky to save energy. Eagles do this by taking advantage of thermals, which are rising currents of warm air. Once an eagle catches a thermal, the bird can glide without flapping its wings. In fact, spreading its long, broad wings wide is the only way an eagle can take advantage of this moving air. To cover long distances, an eagle can glide from one thermal to the next.

You might be surprised to learn that an eagle's tail feathers also play an important role in flight. The bird spreads its tail feathers wide to catch the **updraft** of a rising thermal. The eagle also spreads its tail to slow down as it comes in for a landing.

▶ **The eagle tucks its feet up while it flies.**

CHAPTER 2

Eagles Want a Beach House

Bald eagles can live almost anywhere.
Currently about 70,000 of these birds live in Canada and across the United States, in every state except Hawaii. The state where the most (and biggest) bald eagles live is Alaska, where it can get really cold. Bald eagles are protected by 7,000 feathers that are lined with **down**. The feathers keep the eagles warm—and keep them from getting too hot! To change its body temperature, the bird just has to change the position of its feathers.

Regardless of where they live, bald eagles prefer a certain type of **habitat**—one that is near open water. Why? Bald eagles really like to eat fish, such as salmon, herring, shad, and catfish. They are called sea eagles, after all! Ideally, the eagle's habitat will also include lots of tall trees from which they can look out for prey.

▶ **The Kenai Peninsula in Alaska is a great hunting spot for eagles.**

Gone Fishing

A bald eagle can spot a fish from up to 1 mi. (1.6 km) away. When it does, the powerful predator swoops down at high speed. When it is right over the swimming fish, the eagle spreads its wings to brake. Then it drives its talons into the fish's back and grasps it in its feet. This fierce hunter seldom misses.

The eagle flaps very hard to lift its meal into midair. The eagle will fly to its nest if the fish isn't too heavy. If the fish is too heavy, the eagle carries its meal to shore and eats all it can on the spot. If necessary, the bird can store as much as 2 lb. (0.9 kg) of raw fish in its **crop** to digest later.

Bald eagles sometimes wade into shallow water to catch fish. They have even been seen swimming, using their wings as paddles.

◄ Bald eagles often go into deep water to catch their prey.

Also on the Menu

Although bald eagles prefer fresh fish, they are not picky eaters. They also eat snakes, waterfowl, and turtles. Bald eagles are opportunistic feeders. They eat any kind of flesh, including carrion. Bald eagles pick at dead whales and seals so stinky and gross that other predators won't touch them. They eat roadkill—animals such as squirrels, opossums, and deer that have been run over by cars—even if it has been rotting for days.

Bald eagles also seize any chance to steal food from other birds of prey, like ospreys. The eagle watches from high on its perch and waits for the other bird to kill its prey. Then the eagle swoops in and steals it! The osprey doesn't stand a chance.

Interestingly, though, some smaller birds do fight back. Littler birds, like magpies, can fly in tighter circles than a big eagle can. They peck at and pester the eagle as it flies until finally the eagle leaves them alone.

▶ Bald eagles will grab a meal wherever they can!

Salmon

Fish, like these salmon, make up at least 50% of a bald eagle's diet.

Turtles

▶ Bald eagles seem to like eating turtles more than any other reptile.

Rabbits

Small mammals such as rabbits make up a small portion of an eagle's diet.

Puffins

After fish, puffins and other waterbirds are an eagle's favorite prey.

CHAPTER 3

Becoming a Mom and Dad

When bald eagles reach four or five years old, they are ready to **mate**. Then a female and male will begin a **courtship**. They fly together. They sit on their perches looking for fish together. And as their relationship progresses, they call out to each other as they hunt. To test if their match is a good fit, the pair performs an incredible "dance" while soaring high in the sky. The male and female lock talons and then cartwheel in the air, spinning downward at high speed. Just before reaching the ground, they unhook and fly up again. If this courtship works out, the eagles will mate for life—which can be as long as 20 years in the wild.

▶ Bald eagles test each other to find just the right mate.

Fast Fact
It's possible to watch live video of nesting eagles online.

Choosing a Home

Once a male and female become a pair, they begin to build their nest. This will be a safe place to lay eggs and raise baby eagles. Where will they choose to build their nest?

The eagles look for a high, strong tree near a fishing spot. Ideally, the tree is more than 100 ft. (30.5 m) tall. It's like a castle in the sky. This high nest is called an **aerie**. If the eagles can't find a tree, they'll build their nest in a bush or even on the ground.

A bald eagle's nesting site is at the center of its **territory**. If the area contains a lot of prey, the territory may be relatively small—other eagles' nests might be just a mile away. If there is not a lot of prey in the area, the territory will be larger. And the eagles will defend it vigorously!

◀ This eagle has made its nest in prime real estate—right next to a great fishing spot.

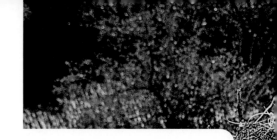

The Biggest Nest

The average-sized eagle nest is 4 to 5 ft. (1.2 to 1.5 m) around and 2 to 4 ft. (0.6 to 1.2 m) deep. The world's biggest bald eagle nest was in Florida. It was 9.5 ft. (2.9 m) around and 20 ft. (6.1 m) deep. It weighed almost 3 tons!

The bald eagle pair builds slowly at first, taking up to three months to make the nest. The birds use their powerful talons to pick up sticks and weave them together. When the female eagle is ready to mate and lay her eggs, the pair packs in a layer of soft moss and leaves to line the inside of the nest.

If a nest is successful—meaning that eggs were hatched—the pair will return to it year after year. That's why some eagle nests are so huge. Every year the eagles add about 1 or 2 ft. (0.3 or 0.6 m) to their nest.

▶ This gigantic eagle nest is in Everglades National Park in Florida.

Fast Fact
An eagle's head
and tail feathers turn
white by age five.

Egg to Eaglet

Mating season differs depending on where an eagle lives, but it usually happens during late fall and winter. The mother eagle lays two or three eggs, and both she and the father take turns **incubating** them.

The parents also have to protect the eggs from predators such as owls, other eagles, and even raccoons. After about 35 days, the eggs are ready to hatch. The baby eagles, called eaglets, use a special egg tooth to break through the shell. Often, the first egg hatches days before the second egg opens up. This gives the firstborn eagle an advantage. The first eaglet makes a big noise, and the parents pay attention. They feed it constantly. When the second eaglet hatches, it gets less attention. Worse still, the second eaglet may be attacked and even killed by its older brother or sister!

Baby eagles don't look at all like adults. They are covered in light gray feathers and look kind of fuzzy. After about three weeks, the eaglets' feathers turn brown.

◀ **Eagle hatchlings
are totally dependent
on their parents
for protection.**

Growing Up

Young eagles need a tremendous amount of food. Some eat 2 lb. (0.9 kg) of fish each day. One of the parents watches over the eaglets while the other hunts for food. The parents tear the fish into bite-sized pieces and feed it to the babies until they learn to tear up the food themselves. That happens when they are about 40 days old. By the time the eaglets are 60 days old, they have already reached full size.

At about 50 days old, the juvenile eagles are ready to begin testing their flight skills. After their first early flights, the eagles return to the nest to eat and sleep. Their parents will continue to feed them for up to 10 weeks. Then the eagles are on their own—literally. They wander through different areas and live by themselves until they are ready to find mates and build their own nests.

▶ Eaglets grow by about 1 lb. (0.5 kg) every four days.

CHAPTER 4

Ancient Eagles

It may seem hard to imagine, but birds **evolved** from **reptiles** about 150 million years ago. Scientists believe the best link between reptiles and birds was *Archaeopteryx*, a birdlike dinosaur that lived during the Jurassic period. The dinosaur was about 1.7 ft. (5.2 m) long and had teeth like a reptile's. It also had a feathered tail and wings, and had claws on its wings.

The first eagles appeared on Earth about 36 million years ago. There were two types: booted eagles and kites. Booted eagles had feathers below their knees. Kites and their descendants, the sea eagles, hunted fish and scavenged for food—and didn't have any feathers on their feet. It was from these birds that bald eagles evolved. Scientists don't know exactly when bald eagles first appeared. The earliest **fossils** they've found for this high flier date back about a million years.

▶ This fossil of an *Archaeopteryx* was found in Germany.

Seafaring Cousins

Golden eagles, which also live in North America, look a lot like juvenile bald eagles. Both are powerful birds of prey that have large wingspans and a lot of brown feathers. However, the two **species** are not closely related. The bald eagle's closest relatives are other fish eaters that include the African fish-eagle and the white-tailed sea eagle.

The African fish-eagle is found throughout sub-Saharan Africa. It has a mostly brown body with black wings and a white head, chest, and tail feathers. The white-tailed sea eagle, which lives across much of Europe and Asia, is mostly brown with white tail feathers. This bird has the largest wingspan of any eagle.

All of these raptors are excellent at hunting fish. They are powerful fliers and have strong talons and sharp beaks. And, like all sea eagles, they have spicules on their toes that enable them to hold on to fish.

◀ White-tailed sea eagles don't hesitate to steal food from one another.

CHAPTER 5

Eagles and Humans

Bald eagles play an important role in the lives of many Native American cultures. These high fliers are seen as a symbol of strength and courage. Their feathers are given to honor great achievements. And in many cultures, eagle bones and feathers are used in **rituals** such as the Sun Dance. Although it is illegal in America to own bald eagle feathers, this doesn't apply to Native Americans.

Like the bald eagle itself, people who have this bird as their **totem** or spirit animal are said to have great vision. They are often tribal or spiritual leaders. Many family groups, or clans, are also named for the bald eagle. Because it was a **sacred** animal, Native Americans never killed the bald eagle for food or sport. The same could not be said of the people who came to America from Europe.

▶ Totem poles are Native American carvings. This one features an eagle head.

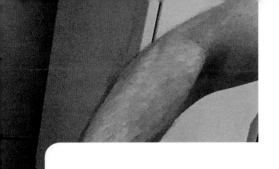

Almost Extinct

It is estimated that there were close to half a million bald eagles in North America in the 1700s. Yet over the next 200 years, they were driven nearly to **extinction**. Their decline was caused entirely by European settlers who came to America.

The settlers saw eagles as competition for food sources, such as fish. Some blamed eagles for killing farm animals. People started shooting eagles on sight. In some states, the government even gave a reward to hunters for each eagle they killed. It is believed that more than 100,000 eagles were shot for money between 1917 and 1952. In 1967, bald eagle numbers had dropped so low that they were placed on the U.S. Fish and Wildlife Service's list of endangered species. It became illegal to kill or harm bald eagles. But these majestic birds still faced other threats.

◀ It is no longer legal to hunt bald eagles, yet this bird is being treated for a gunshot wound.

Ongoing Threats

DDT is a **pesticide** that came into use in the years after World War II. It was sprayed over the land in large amounts. The chemicals seeped into the ground and into water, where they were ingested by fish and other animals that eagles eat. As the chemicals built up in the eagles' bodies, they weakened their eggs. The bald eagles were unable to **reproduce** as they should.

It was only after DDT was banned in 1972 that bald eagles began to recover. Today there are about 70,000 bald eagles in North America. They were taken off the list of Endangered Animals in 2007. But they still face threats from humans.

Like just about every other animal on the planet, the bald eagle suffers from habitat loss. In some areas, overfishing by humans has greatly reduced the fish supply for eagles. Bald eagles are also at risk of being hit by cars, electrocuted by power lines, and struck by wind turbines. It's up to us to protect our environment and the animals that share it.

▶ Farmers still rely on pesticides to protect their crops.

A Powerful Symbol

More than 200 years ago, when America's founders were looking for a symbol for our new country, they chose the bald eagle. They made the bald eagle our national bird and placed it on the Great Seal of the United States. There, the eagle holds arrows in one foot and an olive branch in the other. That shows that our country can be both fierce and peaceful.

Like the Native American peoples before them, the nation's founders saw that the bald eagle was strong and free. They hoped that our country, and the American people, would share the same qualities.

Today, thanks to the efforts of **conservationists**, the bald eagle is still strong and free. It is up to all of us to make sure it stays that way.

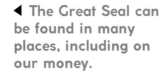

◀ The Great Seal can be found in many places, including on our money.

Bald Eagle Family Tree

Bald eagles belong to the class Aves, also known as birds. All birds have feathers and beaks, and they lay eggs with hard shells. They all have a common ancestor that lived about 150 million years ago. This diagram shows how eagles are related to other birds, such as hawks, vultures, and falcons. The closer together two animals are on the tree, the more similar they are.

Hawks
sharp-sighted hunters with curved beaks and powerful talons to kill prey

Owls
nighttime hunters with exceptional hearing to track their prey

Falcons
some of the fastest animals on Earth; kill prey with their sharp beaks

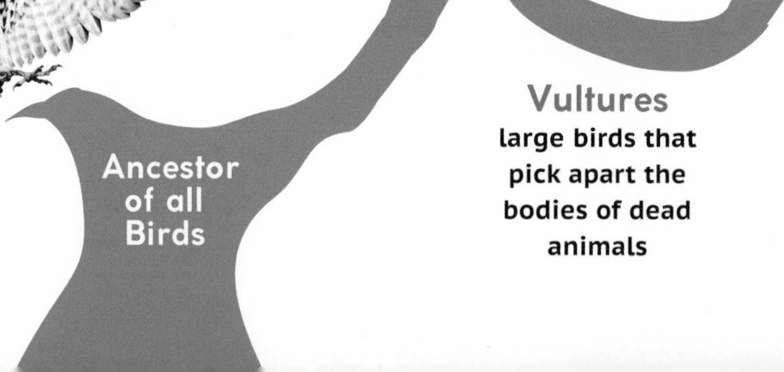

Vultures
large birds that pick apart the bodies of dead animals

Ancestor of all Birds

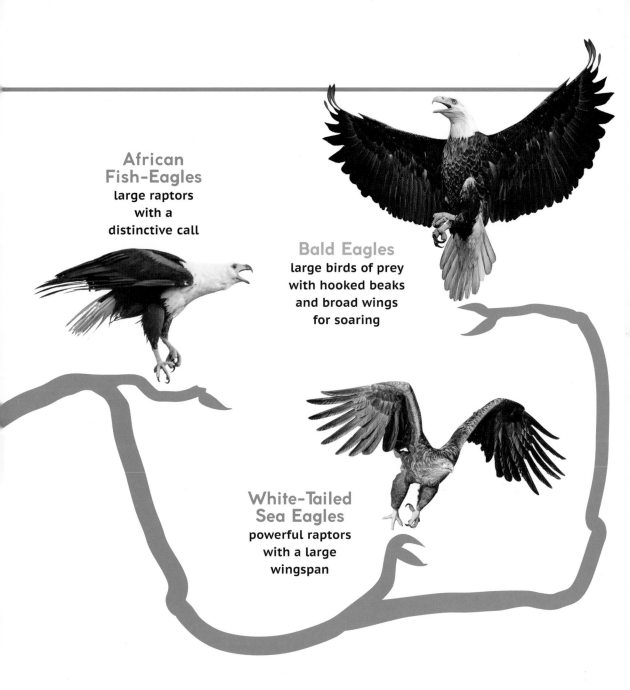

African Fish-Eagles
large raptors with a distinctive call

Bald Eagles
large birds of prey with hooked beaks and broad wings for soaring

White-Tailed Sea Eagles
powerful raptors with a large wingspan

Note: Animal photos are not to scale.

Words to Know

A .... **aerie** *(air-EE)* a large nest of a bird of prey, especially an eagle, typically built high in a tree or on a cliff or mountaintop

C .... **carrion** *(KA-ree-en)* the flesh of dead animals

conservationists *(kahn-sur-VAY-shun-ists)* people who protect valuable things, especially forests, wildlife, or natural resources

courtship *(KORT-ship)* the behavior of birds and other animals aimed at attracting a mate

crop *(KRAHP)* the pouch in a bird's throat where food is stored or prepared for digestion

D .... **down** *(DOUN)* the soft feathers of a bird

E .... **evolved** *(i-VAHLVD)* changed slowly and naturally over time

extinction *(ik-STINGK-shun)* condition of having died out

F .... **fossils** *(FAH-suhls)* bones, shells, or other traces of an animal or plant from millions of years ago, preserved as rock

H .... **habitat** *(HAB-i-tat)* the place where an animal or plant is usually found

I .... **incubating** *(ING-kyuh-bayt-ing)* keeping eggs warm before they hatch

M.......... **mate** *(MATE)* to join together for breeding

P .... **perch** *(PURCH)* a bar or branch on which a bird can rest

pesticide *(PES-ti-side)* a chemical used to kill pests, such as insects

predators *(PRED-uh-tuhrs)* animals that live by hunting other animals for food

prey *(PRAY)* an animal that is hunted by another animal for food

R............ **raptor** *(RAP-tuhr)* a bird of prey

reproduce *(ree-pruh-DOOS)* to produce offspring or individuals of the same kind

reptiles *(REP-tilez)* cold-blooded animals that crawl across the ground or creep on short legs; they have backbones and most reproduce by laying eggs

rituals *(RIH-choo-uhlz)* series of acts that are always performed in the same way, usually as part of a religious or social ceremony

S............ **sacred** *(SAY-krid)* holy, or having to do with religion

soar *(SOR)* to fly or rise high in the air

species *(SPEE-sheez)* one of the groups into which animals and plants are divided; members of the same species can mate and have offspring

T............ **talons** *(TAL-unz)* sharp claws of a bird such as an eagle, hawk, or falcon

territory *(TER-i-tor-ee)* an area that an animal or group of animals uses and defends

totem *(TOH-tem)* an animal, plant, or other natural object that represents a family or clan

traits *(TRAYTS)* qualities or characteristics that make one person or thing different from another

U............ **updraft** *(UHP-draft)* an upward movement of air

Find Out More

BOOKS

- Gray, Susan H. *Bald Eagle (Road to Recovery)*. North Mankato, MN: Cherry Lake Publising, 2009.
- Rose, Deborah Lee, and Jane Veltkamp. *Beauty and the Beak: How Science, Technology, and a 3-D Printed Beak Rescued a Bald Eagle*. Apex, NC: Cornell Lab Publishing Group, 2017.
- Waxman, Laura Hamilton. *Bald Eagles: Prey-Snatching Birds (Comparing Animal Traits)*. Minneapolis, MN: Lerner Publishing Group, 2016.

WEB PAGES

- www.nationaleaglecenter.org

  Meet rescued bald eagles at the National Eagle Center.
- www.allaboutbirds.org/guide/Bald_Eagle/overview

  Learn to identify bald eagles at this site from the Cornell Lab of Ornithology.
- https://explore.org/livecams/bald-eagles/channel-islands-national-park-sauces-bald-eagle

  Click on a LiveCam to watch bald eagles in the wild.

Facts for Now

Visit this Scholastic Web site for more information on bald eagles:
www.factsfornow.scholastic.com Enter the keywords Bald Eagles

Index

A

ancestors 30, *31*

B

beaks 6, *9*, 33

body parts *9*

C

conservation 41

courtship 20, *21*

crop.................................*9*, 17

D

diet......... 5, 6, *7*, 8, *10*, 11, 14, *16*, 17, 18, *19*, 23, 28, *29*, 38

distribution 6, 14, *15*

diving speed 17

down 14

E

eaglets *5*, *26*, 27, 28, *29*

eggs 23, 24, *25*, 27, 38

endangered species list 37

evolution 30

extinction 37

eyesight 8, *9*, 17

F

feathers 14, *26*, 27, 30, 33, 34

flying.................. 6, *7*, 12, *13*, 17, 18, 20

fossils 30, *31*

H

habitat............................... 14, *15*, 38

hallux 11

hunting 8, *15*, 17, 28, 30, 33, *36*, 37

I

incubation 27

M

mating....................20, *21*, 24, 27, 28

N

Native Americans 34, *35*, 41

nests...................*5*, 17, *22*, 23, 24, *25*, 28

P

perches..............................11, 18, 20

predators........................8, 17, 18, 27

prey........... 5, 6, *7*, 8, *10*, 14, *16*, 17, 18, *19*, 23, 28, 38

R

raptors 6, 33

relatives...............................*32*, 33

Index *(continued)*

reproduction 38

S

sacred animals 34

sea eagles 4, 14, 30, *32*, 33

size and weight 5, 8

species 33

speed 12, 17

spiricules 33

stealing food 18

swimming 17

symbols *40*, 41

T

talons 6, 8, *9*, *10*, 11, 17, 20, 24, 33

territory 23

thermals 12

threats 34, *36*, 37, 38, *39*

About the Author

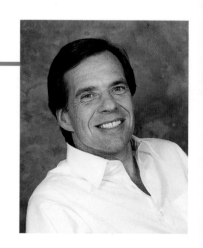

Dr. Hugh Roome is the publisher of *Scholastic News*, *Science World*, and *The New York Times Upfront*. He holds a doctorate from Tufts University. This book is dedicated to the staff of the Tufts Wildlife Clinic at the Cummings School of Veterinary Medicine, where Hugh is a member of the Board of Advisors.